Grid Computing Database

A case of the Oracle Database

Dr. Peter I. Archibong

By

February 24, 2015

Grid Computing Oracle Database

The Grid Computing Information Centre (GRID Infoware, 2004) aimed to promote the development and advancement of technologies that provide seamless and scalable access to wide-area distributed resources. Computational Grids enable the sharing, selection, and aggregation of a wide variety of geographically distributed computational resources (such as supercomputers, compute clusters, storage systems, data sources, instruments, and people) and presents them as a single, unified resource for solving large-scale computing and data intensive computing applications. The new Oracle Database and Oracle Application Server offer a complete software platform designed for Grid Computing (Oracle, 2004). The author compares and contrasts the latest technology of Grid Computing and "Oracle database" implementation. Then the author evaluates the potential utility Oracle Database brings to an IT environment that demands high availability.

Abstract

Grid Computing strives to provide seamless, scalable access to wide-area distributed resources. However, with this benefit of resource collection and distribution, security of that information becomes a major risk (Vijayan, 2004). Currently there is debate among IT professionals as to the security, functionality, middleware, and scalability provisions of computational grids versus Oracle database. The purpose of this paper is to compare and contrast Grid Computing problems, and how Oracle Database addresses these problems. The significance of this paper lies in the fact that 80 percent of computer usage capacity is idle because systems are disjointed and geographically dispersed in organizations. Also, the rate of idle capacity in organizations is growing in an exponential proportion as Moore's Law holds its ground since 1965. The finding of the paper is that the needs for Grid Computing power will very soon become a necessity for organizations as Moore's Law continues to be the guiding principle for IT managers.

Table of Content

Page

Grid Computing: Database Security

Moore's Law will have to fail as silicon matures to the point where innovation stops delivering enhancements in transistor technology. Bradbury (2004) reports that given the amount of money that processor suppliers have invested in technologies that reduce processors' sizes and improve their power, Moore's Law will not fail any time soon. Gordon Moore first created his famous law when he worked for Fairchild Semiconductor Corporation in 1965, three years before he co-founded Intel Corporation. High-performance server configurations have always been about getting multiple systems working in parallel to compensate for limitations in processor technology (Bradbury, 2004). For instance, particle physics experiments at the Large Hadron Collider (LHC), produces 15 Peta-bytes of data each year. To deal with this vast volume of data, particle physicists worldwide have been building a computing Grid. By 2007, this Grid will have the equivalent of 100,000 of today's fastest computers working together to produce a 'virtual supercomputer', which can be expanded and developed as needed (PhysOrg, 2005). As particle physics are producing about 15 peta-bytes of data, Oracle Database is developed to handle data of this magnitude and beyond. Vaas (2003) reports that testers of Oracle Database said that it has elements that will make it easier to deploy across grids, such as improved XML handling, enhanced Web services APIs and 8-exabyte file support. The functionality and scalability of Oracle Database is sufficient to handle the data produce by particle physics. To make such extreme scalability possible, Oracle enhanced the Real Application Clusters (RAC) technology in its database, as well as improved the way it distributed SQL statements across a cluster in a blade server farm.

Webopedia (2004) reports that Grid Computing is a form of networking. Also, Grid Computing is a form of distributed computing that involves coordinating and sharing computing, application, data, storage, or network resources across dynamic and geographically dispersed organizations (Grid.org, 2004). Grid technologies offer organizations the ability to tackle complex computational problems with efficiency and security (Grid.org 2004). However, unlike conventional networks that focus on communication among devices, Grid Computing harnesses unused processing cycles of all computers in a network for solving problems too intensive for any stand-alone machine.

A well-known Grid Computing project is the SETI (Search for Extraterrestrial Intelligence) project, in which personal computer users worldwide donated unused processor cycles to help the search for signs of extraterrestrial life by analyzing signals coming from outer space. The project relied on individual users to volunteer and allow the project to harness the unused processing power of the volunteer's computer. This method of Grid Computing was noted to save the project both money and personnel/time resources (Buyya, 2004).

Vijayan (2004) reports that the aforementioned type of Grid Computing tends to magnify security risks. Among the concerns for security with Grid Computing user authentication, authorization and access control, as well as auditing and data integrity enhances security risks when data is in storage and in transit. In addition, viruses and worms are more easily transmitted in Grid Computing set ups (Vijayan, 2004). For industries such as banking, education and business these security issues have been noted, but not solved for public-key infrastructure (PKI)-based or Kerberos-based Grid Computing.

In a PKI-based infrastructure environment, servers and clients mutually authenticate each other using digital certificates issued by a trusted authority. In a Kerberos setup, the same thing could be accomplished via encrypted keys stored in advance on a Kerberos authentication server. However, both of these Grid Computing set ups have many security risks previously identified. Therefore, Vijayan (2004) suggested that other Grid Computing set ups that include the use of Secure Sockets Layer technology. Secure Sockets Layer technology authenticates servers by clients before starting an encrypted session (Vijayan, 2004).

Standards for efficiency, security and set-up have been in the development phase for some time now, and the arrival of Oracle Grid Computing offers security solutions that others do not offer. The paper compares and contrasts standard Grid Computing with Oracle Database which promotes additional security, availability, searching, and scalability features for the IT environment. This analysis will assist IT professionals in determining objectively the best Grid Computing solutions for their needs.

Traditional Grid Computing Analysis

Cuenca (2004) researched the Traditional Grid Planet2 that comprised of 3000 University students sharing over 20 tera-bytes (TB) of information. Cuenca (2004) found numerous problems with traditional Grid Computing in the form of inadequate security, poor data availability, searching by root directory shared-folders caused difficulties to find unpopular references, and poor scalability. In addition, Li (2004) reports that Grid Computing has received widespread attention in recent years as a significant new research field regarding grid system security; the two major issues are: (a) authentication; and (b) authorization. The majority of existing research has taken place in the authentication arena. To date, there has been only limited work on the grid system authorization problem which Oracle Database is touted to solve. Previous researchers found four major problems with traditional Grid Computing; therefore IT managers should be cognizant of these problems and compare to see how Oracle Database or other applications solve these problems of security, data availability, searching and scalability.

Grid Security

The lack of adequate security with traditional Grid Computing is a serious problem, given its heterogeneous and geographical security vulnerability. Lorch (2004) reports that computational grids and other heterogeneous, large-scale distributed systems require more powerful and more flexible authorization mechanisms to realize fine-grained access-control of resources. Usage scenarios for advanced grids require support for small, dynamic working groups, direct delegation of access privileges among users, procedures for establishing trust relationships without requiring organizational level agreements, precise management by individuals of their privileges, and retention of authority by resource providers. Lorch (2004) further noted that existing systems fail to provide the necessary flexibility and granularity to support these scenarios. The reasons include the overhead imposed by required administrator intervention, coarse granularity that only allows for all-or-nothing access control decisions, and the inability to implement finer-grained access control without requiring trusted application code.

The authentication and authorization security features previously mentioned in reference to Oracle Database are not available on the predecessor Grid Computing setups which are often PKI-based or Kerberos-based. In these Grid Computing setups, which are based on a public-key infrastructure (PKI) environment, servers and clients could mutually authenticate each other using digital certificates issued by a trusted authority. In a Kerberos setup, the same thing could be accomplished via encrypted keys stored in advance on a Kerberos authentication server. Other methods include the use of Secure Sockets Layer technology to authenticate servers by clients before starting an encrypted session. However, these features fall short of their security intention regarding authentication and authorization as information continues to be at risk and virus/worm attacks are possible (Vijayan, 2004).

Grid Availability

Data availability is a problem in the traditional Grid Computing. It uses manual replication by users based on popularity of data. Upgrading from low 24 percent to high availability 99 percent required by Internet will be prohibitively expensive (Cuenca, 2004). Grid Computing set ups are increasingly used for collaborative problem-solving and advanced science and engineering applications.

Mizan (2004) reports that Grid Computing is an emerging computing paradigm to execute applications across geographically distributed shared resources. Grid applications usually have strict quality of service (QoS) requirements which must be met with guaranteed resource allocation. Furthermore, a Grid application may have multiple component tasks that run simultaneously on different resources. Performance of such Grid applications not only depends on the proper resource co-allocation but also on performance isolation and coordinated usage of allocated resources. Therefore it is necessary for Grid resource management architecture to incorporate functionalities for ensuring coordinated resource usage during the execution of a multi-component Grid application (Mizan, 2004).

Grid Searching

Using root directory key shared data is a limitation for both data search and retrieval in the traditional Grid Computing. Searching across a subset of online grid communities in most traditional grids will result in uncontrolled file availability and items not found errors. Limitation of traditional grid in terms of finding unpopular references because researching relied on root directory key shared data is a serious problem. Traditional grid relied on retrieval techniques of crawling to build a centralized index and spent enormous resources polling for updates to be able to keep up with dynamicity of Internet search (Ceunca, 2004).

Wang (2004) reports that traditional Grid Computing enabled the coordinated sharing of large-scale distributed heterogeneous computing resources that can be used to solve computationally intensive problems in science, engineering, and commerce. Grid applications are made possible by high-speed networks and a new generation of Grid middleware that resides between networks and traditional applications. In terms of searching using its root directory key method traditional grid is not efficient searching across heterogeneous middleware and geographically disperse cluster servers.

Grid Scalability

Cheruvu (2004) stated that Grid Computing is a framework for resource sharing across multiple organizations, and operating in different administrative domains. Grids are built over wide-area networks. They provide infrastructure for wide-area distributed computing platforms. Grids provide secure and fine-grained access to computational resources in multiple organizational domains that require scalability.

Min (2001) states that Grid requirement of quality of service (QoS) in the resource management is a top priority in selecting Grid Computing infrastructure. The quality of service (QoS) requirement specifies that Grid should finish any work sent in at a specified amount of time and also to perform at least above average level of service for each production cycle. Grid Computing is considered to be a classic versatile system in terms of better handling of jobs arrival and departure and their resources. Therefore, early resources scheduling is mandatory in the Grid system environment to ensure their availability to meet the needs of different tasks. Min (2001) however stated that these quality and volume requirements cannot be guaranteed with traditional Grid Computing applications involving PKI, Kerberos, and Secure Sockets Layer technology. Therefore, solutions to the security authentication and authorization shortcomings, grid availability, grid content and dynamic searching, and grid scalability as reported by Cuenca (2004) and Li (2004) as the major problems of the traditional Grid Computing, are proposed by Oracle Database.

Oracle Database Analysis

Oracle Database responded to the security shortcomings of PKI, Kerberos and Secure Socket Layer technology by adding Content Services Database repository for unstructured content with improved Windows desktop access and Web interface, folder- and document-level security, group- and role-based access control, and automatic policy-based versioning (Solheim, 2005). Oracle Database Release 2.0 includes features designed to help companies more easily manage data and comply with data-protection regulations (Whiting, 2005). Oracle Database Release 2.0 is the latest version of Grid Computing database with improved data-management and backup capabilities.

Oracle Database Security

Oracle database Grid Computing is designed with improved security as reported by Lorch (2004). Oracle introduces centralized security and authentication to break the barrier of fragmented security problem in the IT infrastructure (Demarest, 2003). These security upgrades however do not isolate and coordinate usage of allocated resources which would limit the functionality or efficiency of this Grid Computing method.

Some of the new features are also designed to help companies comply with the data-protection requirements mandated by the Sarbanes-Oxley Act and other governmental regulations (Whiting, 2005). As of September 2005, 30,000 customers have changed to Oracle Database Release 2, because of its improved security (Whiting, 2005). The improved Oracle Database security features include: (a) Automated Storage Management system; and (b) Oracle's Real Application Clusters (RAC) clustering technology. The updated Oracle Database RAC can manage up to 100 servers and also encrypt specific columns in data tables.

Oracle Database Availability

According to Min (2001), Oracle Database Grid Computing is designed for high availability or near zero down time. Specifically, Oracle Database is the first database Grid Computing software that can produce over one million transactions per minutes continuously with a near zero downtime. Oracle Database software has the ability to finish any work sent in at a specified amount of time, and resources rescheduling enhances the speed of transactions (TPC, 2003). In addition, Brixius (2000) reports that Oracle database Grid Computing exceeded this performance need by being able to handle large distributed database with 99 percent availability or near zero down time made possible by its advance Real Application Clusters (RAC) system. For example, Oracle Database automated features enhance speed and reliability, and availability to produce over one million transactions per minutes (TPC, 2003). Also, Oracle database Grid automated features such as memory management, storage management, self-diagnosis, centralized configuration and patch management capabilities, allow Database Administrators to manage large, complex environments with very little interference (McCown, 2005). Finally, Oracle Database RAC runs applications faster than the fastest mainframe, and if a server fails, the traditional grid stops while Oracle Database RAC keeps running. When adding more processing power, simply add another server without taking users offline (Milne, 2005). Oracle Database provides redundancy and failover protection.

Oracle Database Searching

Advanced dynamic and content searching is a major improvement in Oracle Database computing. Wang (2004) reports that Oracle database Grid Computing comes with enhanced search engines that relies on content search and ranking and provides dynamic search engine. This dynamic search engine can traverse the Oracle Database Automatic Storage Management that can coordinate up to 100 servers with its embedded middleware. In addition, Oracle Database database Grid Computing is more effective than traditional Grid Computing MEG applications as reported by Azzedin (2001). Specifically, Oracle Application Server Database Multimedia Tag Library for JSP is an extension of Oracle "interMedia" Java Classes for "serverlets" and "JavaServer Pages" that simplifies retrieving and uploading media data from and to Oracle Database in multimedia JSP Web applications (Oracle Database Multimedia, 2005).

Oracle Database Scalability

Oracle Database was designed for scalability according to Cheruvu (2004). For example, Oracle database Grid Computing software comes in three packages for unlimited scalability: Standard edition with two maximum processors to handle a small business; Standard edition two with four maximum processors for medium size business, and finally, the Enterprise edition that comes with unlimited number of processors and clustering servers that span regions, countries and continents.

In addition, Min (2001) reports that Oracle Database is made up of low cost modular components, low incremental costs, and no single point of failure. Oracle Database's features provide enterprise services at low cost by harnessing the power of all idle computer systems into a single conglomerate Grid Computing power house efficiently regardless of their physical location. Oracle Database makes it practical to start a small size grid and scale up as needed. For example, Mainstay Partners (2004) reports that Ohio Savings Bank, University of Oslo and Dell Corporation are using Oracle Database. Their specific areas of savings are on computer hardware, software and computing performance improvement.

Traditional Grid Computing versus Oracle Database Summary

Oracle Application Database has five other major features that are related to the advantages over traditional Grid Computing applications in addition to categories of security, availability, searching, and scalability already discussed.

1. Oracle Database provides all the middleware services users need to deploy and manage applications and Web services.

2. Oracle Database database also has the capability to deliver personalized applications through enterprise portals and mobile devices.

3. Oracle Database has the ability to provide real-time business intelligence.

4. Oracle Database can integrate applications, and automates business processes.

5. Oracle Database is optimized to take full advantage of cluster computing and enterprise grid deployment architectures (Oracle Enterprise Manager Concept, 2004).

In support of the advantages Oracle Database offers over traditional Grid Computing methods of PKI, Kerberos and Secure Sockets Layer technology, McCright (2004) reports that Oracle was the first Grid Computing database company to form a consortium of 21 members (Enterprise Grid Alliance (EGA) to continually monitor, research and improve on common security issues that tend to amplify with Grid's geographically distributed infrastructure. Among these members include Sun Microsystems, Inc., Hewlett-Packard Corp., and EMC Corp.

Oracle Methods

To maximize Oracle database Grid Computing software advantages over traditional Grid Computing applications of PKI, Kerberos, and

Secure Socket Layer technology the following six methods were recommended by Oracle (2004):

1. Users should create groups: heterogeneous groups, database groups, and host groups.

2. Users should create specific-groups: (a) database-specific group; (b) host-specific group; and (c) heterogeneous-specific group.

3. Users should create server-groups including Oracle Management Agents, Application Servers, Beacons, Databases, HTTP servers, host-servers, Lightweight Directory Access Protocol (LDAP) Servers, Oracle Management Service and Oracle Management Repository, and Web Applications.

4. Users should create group-functions or a particular function within a company, for example manufacturing, operations, sales, marketing, and human resources.

5. Users should assign target-groups in creating particular administrators.

6. Users should combine targets by types and by maintenance schedule.

Manageability not grid

Monash (2003) reports that manageability, advance data warehousing and business intelligence are the design focuses of Oracle Database and not grid. Grid was adopted a couple of months before product release as a marketing focus. However, Oracle's commitment to cluster and grid technology is real and important. For IT managers who need immediate benefits of Grid Computing by upgrading to Oracle Database, should wait for future releases such as Oracle11g, Orcle12g, etc. For IT managers whose primary need is saving on total cost of ownership (TCO), it makes perfect strategic sense to upgrade to Oracle Database because manageability is historically a major competitive challenge for Oracle; Oracle Database has solved manageability problems.

Common Installation problems

Oracle Database installations may fail because of insufficient disk space, improper permissions, and shared memory problems. First, insufficient disk space; IT managers should study the installation guide before starting the installation process. To create a starter database during the installation, it is important to make sure there is at least four gigabyte of disk space for the binaries alone. Windows installations may require a slightly smaller disk space. For UNIX systems, the Oracle Universal Installer requires up to 600 MB of space in the "/tmp" directory. Second, improper permissions; the installation guide provides a detailed security permissions required to perform a successful installation. Third, shared memory; in UNIX and LINUX operating systems, shared memory and semaphore parameters could also be problems. IT managers should check the system configuration file (/etc/system) in the many UNIX systems and set proper parameters for shared memory and semaphores (Foot, 2005).

Discussion

Potential utility of Grid in the IT environment

One of the IT managers' responsibilities is to research and select the best technology that adds values to organization's information technology management, and improve profitability. One of the latest technologies that can improve profitability immediately is the Grid Computing. Grid Computing is the sharing of processors' computational resources from heterogeneous computers from a private source or public utility source to improve profitability (CSC, 2005). To this endeavor IT manager's is to build a private grid or connect to the public utility grid. There are some short and long-term performance implications in using grid. Short-term performance indicators are in the form of lower computing costs, faster project results, and better product results. The long term implications are customers' satisfaction and high employees' morale and productivity.

Short-term performance implication

Lower Computing Costs: On a price-to-performance basis, a Grid Computing project gets more work done with less administration and budget than dedicated hardware solutions. Depending on the size of the network, the price-to-performance ratio for computing power can literally improve by an order of magnitude. For example, University of Oslo's is using Oracle Database Application server to manage its Web infrastructure for writing and producing Web pages, and for disseminating official university information. Mainstay found that the university immediately lowered costs and improved performance and predicts additional grid's automation (Mikkelsen, 2004).

Faster Project Results

The extra power generated by the Grid Computing can directly impact on an organization's ability to win in the marketplace by shortening product development cycles and accelerating research and development processes. For example, Dell's use of a single clustered database provides fewer moving parts, greater flexibility, and more manageability providing Dell an advantage over competitors in the computer marketplace (Koster, 2004).

Better Product Results

An increased in affordable computing power by grid means not having to ignore promising avenues or solutions because of a limited budget or schedule. The power created by a Grid Computing can help to ensure a higher quality product by allowing higher-resolution testing and results, and can permit an organization to test more extensively prior to product release. For example, Ohio

Saving Bank, invested in Oracle Database Grid Computing to scale resources and provide the support and services; this has given the Ohio Saving a niche in the industry by being able to use grid's higher-resolution testing and results; thereby adding strategic services to their product line such as a better call center, online mortgage processing, and data warehouse applications (Boylan, 2004).

Long term performance implication

Long term performance implication includes a higher customer satisfaction rating due to high quality product resulting from grid's higher-resolution testing. Additionally, the Grid Computing enhances higher employee morals and high level of organizational performance brought about by reduced workload per employee, but higher product quality. For example, University of Oslo experienced a 10 percent increase in enrollment in the Spring of 2004 as compared to 2002, also less number of employees requested sick leave in the student services departments in 2004 as compared to 2002 (Mikkelsen, 2004).

Limitations of Grid Computing

Leon, Amirfathi, Ramanujan, & Srinivasan (2005) report that limitations of the Grid Computing are in the form of technology transition, software implication, complex licensing implication, product implication workload demarcations, and multi-core CPUs.

Technology Transitions implication

Grid is rooted in the high performance clusters (HPC) due to early demands that dictated that technologies and usage models should be HPC, hence cycle scavenging and distributed parallel computation is adopted in grid. Developments like multi-core CPUs may become forced function for the pervasive use of multi-threaded and parallel programming techniques that have been used for 20 years by HPC is now adaptable for Grid Computing. A quantum jump in benefit can be achieved only if grid is adopted in a larger scale (Leon et al., 2005), but there is no performance gains in smaller projects. Therefore, grid is not suitable for an independent small shop.

Software implication

The turning point is reached in the 21st century where extra performance came from an ever-faster-running processor and from the use of functional unit to uncover parallelism within the instruction stream. It also led to increasing heat-dissipation problems. Currently, there are not enough applications on the retail shelf for Grid Computing. However, over a long run, application vendors and consumer will incorporate parallelism into their application solutions as the increase in the multi-core CPU chip drives the price down; there will be more familiarity with parallelism and easier to port applications in grid environment

(Leon et al., 2005). Current applications need to be modified or re-deployed, and worst still, grid is not appropriate for applications that require fast response time.

Complex Licensing implication

Software licensing is very expensive for organizations. Grids can make it more expensive and complicated, and could be a problem in a large scale. It is important for the IT managers to note that per processor licensing in the existing applications not usable in grid environment. New processor licenses are required. In a grid environment scheme, the first program's run can take 10 processors; next run may require 10,000 processors. Therefore, the current software licensing per CPU is not compatible with the grid's multi-core, multi-threaded environment (Leon et al., 2005).

Product Implication

It is important for IT managers to know that Grid is not a product. You can not walk into a store and purchase a grid. Grid-ready, grid-compatible components are not likely in the near future, but grid has to be built. For example, Electric utility company does not acquire grid as a unit; they build grids, and grids evolve over time. It is also possible to acquire a company that already has grids. The character of grid is shaped by business processes that run the grid such as available sources of capital, ownership models, regulatory environment and relationship with subscribers (Leon et al., 2005).

Adoption Size Implication

Small size grid does not yield immediate return on investment (ROI). However, four sizes of grid are available. First, departmental grid can be formed by pulling together dozens of desktops or servers. Second, enterprise grids are made up of pulling together enterprise wide resources. Third, "Extraprise" grids are form with multiple companies contributing resources to a large-scale grid. Finally, global grids are form with users all over the world participating through Internet to form a global grid; for example, SETI@home (Yang, 2004).

Deployment Recommendation

Grid is right for companies that want to run computationally intensive applications at a reduce cost. However, like other new technology before grid, deployment may be very expensive at the onset and security vulnerability may get out of control, but as technology evolves, the implementation cost may reduce considerably. Grid technology is still in its infancy (CSC, 2005) therefore any grid projects should be thoroughly investigated, researched, and analyzed. Grid pilot test projects should be carefully evaluated before a decision is made about enterprise wide implementation. Once the decision is made, there are five steps to deploy grid: Plan computing-power needs, choose type of grid, deploy off-the-shelf products, modify applications for grid, and test the grid.

Plan computation power

IT managers should take inventory of current desktops or servers to be used for creating grid and determine the total computing power. For example, 100 Intel Pentium 4 CPUs, Speed 3GHz, 2-Flop per cycle, and 90% availability will result in 540 computing power (100 x 3 x 2 x .90 = 540). Computing power is needed for setting up grid software. Managing change is important; IT managers should remember to discuss with the technology staff about the new changes such as a department that no longer manages their servers, but merge with the Grid Computing service's central management.

Choose type of grid

There are three type of grid to choose from: supercomputer, cluster computing, and Grid Computing. Supercomputer is a high-end performance computer for running specific programs extremely fast such as nuclear energy research and weather forecast. There is no modification to existing the operating system or applications, if a company selects supercomputer type of grid. However supercomputers are very expensive, and they are not scalable. A Clustering computing is a second option. Clustering is a popular strategy for implementing parallel processing applications because it enables companies to leverage the investment already made in PCs and workstations (Webopedia, 2005). It offers scalable load capacity, no additional operating system and application required. However, clustering is not high performance in terms of program execution time. Building a Grid Computing is the ultimate option. Grid offers high and scalable performance, built from existing infrastructure; but grid applications needs modifications, before it can be re-deployed. Finally, grid is not good for application that requires fast response time (Yang, 2004).

Deploy off-the-shelf products

There are some off-the-shelf grid products beginning to feature in the market. For example United Devices MP offers grid software for Linux, Solaris, Unix and Window 98, Windows NT, Window 2000 and Windows XP. This is best for companies wanting to utilize heterogeneous desktop install-base for Grid Computing.

Modify applications for grid

It is important to determine early if the existing application can be re-deployed for Grid Computing. In order to benefit from Grid Computing, an application must be computationally intensive. For example, application that can handle large amounts of data from many sources, and doing the same thing repeatedly to arrive at a result, is the best for grid deployment. For instance, Oracle Database is deployed for Grid Computing while Oracle 9i is not.

Testing

Testing the Grid Computing scheme is very important regardless of the project, because the test result will guide the decision to grid or not to grid. The grid should speed up as more clients participate, but not linearly. Measure every computer on the grid for signs of under-utilization or over-loading, compare cost against alternative methods. IT manager should verify that the grid application is running accurately, and not just running fast. Also, IT manager should verify that other systems on the network is not adversely affected or employees' productivities are not affect (Yang, 2004)

Conclusion

Companies on the average utilize only 20% of their server capacity and other computer systems, but 80% capacity is idle because systems are disjointed and geographically dispersed. With system components numbering into thousands, it is unrealistic to think that users can manage these components individually. Hence, the application of Grid Computing was born. Oracle Grid Computing software allows large-scale to fine-grained granular control of all components in a geographically dispersed computing environment (Oracle Enterprise Manager Concept, 2004). Oracle Database Database represents a major step forward in the Grid Computing technology. McCown (2005) reports that large operations will definitely find Oracle Database Database advanced characteristics useful for enterprises to manage their database systems. Advantages in every category previously examined (e.g., security, availability, searching and scalability) support this statement. However, IT managers should be aware of common installations problems, savings on enhanced manageability and hope for a better grid product in the future versions of Oracle.

References

Azzedin, F. (2001). *Synchronous queuing: A co-allocation mechanism for multimedia-enabled grids.* Retrieved January 21, 2005 from ProQuest Digital Dissertations (UMI No. AAT MQ62688) http://library.capella.edu:2227/dissertations/fullcit/MQ62688

Bradbury, D. (2004) Making More Of Moore's Law. *Computer Weekly;* 10/5/2004, p34-35, 2p, 1c

Boylan, J. (2004). *Free ROI studies: Ohio savings bank.* Retrieved January 21, 2005 from http://www.oracle.com/technologies/grid/grid_roi.html

Brixius, N. (2000). *Solving large-scale quadratic assignment problems.* Retrieved January 21, 2005 from ProQuest Digital Dissertations (UMI No. AAT 9996075) http://library.capella.edu:2227/dissertations/fullcit/9996075

Buyya, R. (2004). *Grid Computing and distributed systems (GRIDS) laboratory.* Retrieved January 21, 2005 from http://www.gridcomputing.com/gridfaq.html

Cheruvu, P. (2003). *Tuple space computing on the grid.* Retrieved January 21, 2005 from ProQuest Digital Dissertations

http://library.capella.edu:2227/

dissertations/fullcit/EP10344

CSC (2005). *CSC's Grid Computing Solution Provides Flexibility,*
Cost Savings. Retrieved January 21, 2005 from
http://www.csc.com/features/2005/23.shtml

Demarest, G. (2003). *Why Oracle Database is the best platform for*
enterprise Grid Computing. Retrieved January 21, 2005 from
http://www.oracle.com/webapps/
search/search.do?keyword=grid+computing&group=OTNDOCS&group=E
VENTS&group=EBN

Foot, C. (2005). *Oracle Database Binary Installation.* Retrieved
November 11, 2005 from http://www.dbazine.com/blogs/blog-
cf/chrisfoot/ Databasebinaryinstallation

Grid.org. (2004). *Grid Computing.* Retrieved January 21, 2005 from
http://www.grid.org/about/gc/

Monash, C. (2004). The Real Point of Oracle Database –
Manageability. Retrieved November 11, 2005 from
http://www.monash.com/oracle Database.html

McCown, S. (2005). *Database management by automation.* Retrieved
January 21, 2005 from

http://itproductguidebeta.infoworld.com/Oracle_Database_
Database_Release_1/product_47195.html?view=0&curNodeId=0

Koster, B. (2004). *Free ROI studies: Dell Eurostar.* Retrieved January 21, 2005 from http://www.oracle.com/technologies/grid/grid_roi.html

Leon, E., Amirfathi, M., Ramanujan, R., & Srinivasan, K. (2005). Understanding the Platform Requirements of Emerging Enterprise Solutions. *Intel Technology Journal*; May 2005, Vol. 9 Issue 2, p165-174, 10p

Li, J. (2004). *Authorization service for grid system environments.* ProQuest Digital Dissertation (UMI No. AAT 3128168). Retrieved January 21, 2005 from http://library.capella.edu:2227/dissertations/fullcit/3128168

Lorch, M. (2004). *PRIMA: Privilege management and authorization in Grid Computing environments.* Retrieved January 21, 2005 from ProQuest Digital Dissertations. (UMI No. AAT 3123723) http://library.capella.edu:2227/dissertations/fullcit/3123723

Mainstay Partners. (2004). *Oracle Grid Computing customers achieve 150% ROI.* Retrieved January 21, 2005 from http://www.oracle.com/technologies/grid/grid_roi.html

McCright, J. S. (2004). Oracle leads new grid consortium. *eWeek, 21*(17), 37. Retrieved January 21, 2005 from http://search.epnet.com/login.aspx?direct=true&db=buh&an=1301 6353

Milne, D. (2005). *Industry-Leading Scalability and Non-Stop Availability.* Retrieved January 21, 2005 from http://www.oracle.com/database/rac_home.html

Min, R. (2001). *Scheduling advance reservations with priorities in Grid Computing systems.* Retrieved January 21, 2005 from ProQuest Digital Dissertations (UMI No. AATMQ62798). http://library.capella.edu:2227/dissertations/fullcit/MQ62798

Mizan, T. (2004). *Coordinated virtual partition: A resource provisioning framework for grid applications.* Retrieved January 21, 2005 from ProQuest Digital Dissertations (UMI No. AAT MQ91269). http://library.capella.edu:2227/dissertations/fullcit/MQ91269

Oracle. (2004). *Overview of Oracle grid architecture: Oracle® Database Documentation* Database Release 1 (10.1), Part Number B10743-01.

Oracle® Enterprise Manager Concepts. (2004). Retrieved January 21, 2005 from http://oraclesvca2.oracle.com/ docs/cd/B14117_01/em.101/b12016/toc.htm

Oracle Database Multimedia. (2005). *Oracle® application server Database multimedia tag library for JSP user's guide and reference Database (9.0.4) Part No. B10445-01*. Retrieved January 21, 2005 from http://www.oracle.com/ technology/products/intermedia/htdocs/jsptaglib/html/title.ht m

PhysOrg (2005) *World's Largest Working Computing Grid*. Retrieved January 21, 2005 from http://www.physorg.com/news1061.html

Solheim, S. (2005). Oracle Database collaboration suite finding its niche. *eWeek, 22*(33), 11-12.

TPC. (2005). *Top ten TPC-C by performance*: *Transaction processing council (TPC)*. Retrieved January 21, 2005 from http://www.tpc.org/tpcc/results/ tpcc_perf_results.asp

Vaas, L. (2003). Oracle Database geared for the grid. (cover story). *eWeek*; 8/04/2003, Vol.

20 Issue 31, p1, 2p, 1c

Vijayan, J. (2004). Guarding the Grid. *Computerworld, 38*(48), 32-
    33.

Whiting,   R.   (2004).   Oracle   shoots   for   database   lead.
    InformationWeek, 1044, 54-57. Retrieved January 21, 2005 from
    http://search.epnet.com/login.aspx?direct=true&db=aph&an=1743
    3212

Wang,   S.   (2004).   *Grid-based   geo-middleware   for   geographic*
    analysis: Theory,   method,   implementation,   and   evaluation.
    Retrieved   January   21,   2005   from   ProQuest   Digital
    Dissertations   (UMI   No.   AAT   3139402).
    http://library.capella.edu:2227/dissertations/fullcit/3139402

Webopedia. (2004). *Grid Computing.* Retrieved January 21, 2005 from
    http://webopedia.com/TERM/g/ grid_computing.html

Yang, J. (2004). Project Map Deploying a Grid-Computing System.
    Baseline; Feb2004 Issue 27, p72-73, 2p, 3 charts, 1 diagram

www.ingramcontent.com/pod-product-compliance
Lightning Source LLC
Chambersburg PA
CBHW041153050326
40690CB00001B/465